Principles of safeguarding and protection for learning disability workers

Series Editor: Lesley Barcham

Mandatory Unit and Common Induction Standards titles

Communicating effectively with people with a learning disability
ISBN 978 0 85725 510 5

Personal development for learning disability workers ISBN 978 0 85725 609 6

Equality and inclusion for learning disability workers ISBN 978 0 85725 514 3

Duty of care for learning disability workers ISBN 978 0 85725 613 3

Principles of safeguarding and protection for learning disability workers
ISBN 978 0 85725 506 8

Person centred approaches when supporting people with a learning disability
ISBN 978 0 85725 625 6

Principles of safeguarding and protection for learning disability workers

Simon Bickerton

Supporting the level 2 and 3 Diplomas in
Health and Social Care (learning disability pathway)
and the Common Induction Standards

LearningMatters

bild
all about people

Acknowledgements

Photographs from www.crocodilehouse.co.uk. Our thanks to Sophie and Marianne and to Choices Housing and Autism Plus for their help.

First published in 2011 jointly by Learning Matters Ltd and the British Institute of Learning Disabilities

British Library Cataloguing in Publication Data
A CIP record for this book is available from the British Library

ISBN: 978 0 85725 506 8
This book is also available in the following ebook formats:
Adobe ebook ISBN: 978 0 85725 508 2
EPUB ebook ISBN: 978 0 85725 507 5
Kindle ISBN: 978 0 85725 509 9

Cover design by Pentacor
Text design by Pentacor
Project Management by Deer Park Productions, Tavistock
Typeset by Pantek Arts Ltd, Maidstone
Printed and bound in Great Britain by Ashford Colour Press Ltd, Gosport, Hants.

Learning Matters Ltd
20 Cathedral Yard
Exeter
EX1 1HB
Tel: 01392 215560
E-mail: info@learningmatters.co.uk
www.learningmatters.co.uk

BILD
Campion House
Green Street
Kidderminster
Worcestershire
DY10 1JL
Tel: 01562 723010
E-mail: enquiries@bild.org.uk
www.bild.org.uk

Contents

This book covers:

- Common Induction Standards – Standard 6 – Principles of safeguarding in health and social care
- Level 2 and level 3 diploma units HSC 024 – Principles of safeguarding and protection in health and social care.

About the author and the people who contributed to this book

Simon

Simon has spent the last 28 years working in health and social care. He has worked as both a general and mental health nurse, and has also worked for a local authority, which has involved working in a mental health crisis service, managing mental health day services and then managing community-based services for adults with learning disabilities. While working for the local authority, Simon achieved the Certificate in Education and the NVQ4 Registered Manager award.

Simon now works as a freelance trainer. This involves working with a number of different services and organisations around the country, training staff and helping to develop the quality of services. Simon has worked with BILD for about six years.

Simon is married, has four children and he lives in the north west of England.

Karen and Bill

Karen Flood and Bill Heron contributed stories about their own experiences and those of other people with learning disabilities.

Karen and Bill are directors of First Step, which is a not-for-profit organisation based in Liverpool. First Step aims to support its members to speak out and challenge poor practice and injustices. They both have learning disabilities and have personal experience of support services.

Other contributors

Two other people have contributed and have asked not to be named.

One of these is the safeguarding manager from an English local authority, who has provided information about how the evaluation of safeguarding processes led to the development of much easier to follow policy and procedures.

The other person is a manager from health services, who has provided a story that describes the benefits and difficulties involved in reporting the bad practice of colleagues.

Introduction

Who is this book for?

Principles of Safeguarding and Protection for Learning Disability Workers is for you if you:

- have a new job working with people with learning disabilities with a support provider or as a personal assistant;

- are a more experienced worker who is studying for a qualification for your own professional development or are seeking more information to improve your practice;

- are a volunteer supporting people with a learning disability;

- are a manager in a service supporting people with a learning disability and you have training or supervisory responsibility for the induction of new workers and the continuous professional development of more experienced staff;

- if you are a direct payment or personal budget user and are planning the induction or training for your personal assistant.

Links to qualifications and the Common Induction Standards

This book gives you all the information you need to complete both one of the Common Induction Standards and the unit on principles of safeguarding and protection from the level 2 and level 3 diplomas in health and social care. You may use the learning from this unit in a number of ways:

- to help you complete the Common Induction Standards;

- to work towards a full qualification e.g. the level 2 or level 3 diploma in health and social care;

- as learning for the unit on safeguarding and protection for your professional development.

This unit is one of the mandatory units that everyone doing the full level 2 and level 3 diploma must study. Although anyone studying for the qualifications will find the book useful, it is particularly helpful for people who support a person with a learning disability. The messages and stories used in this book are from people with a learning disability, family carers and people working with them.

Links to assessment

If you are studying for this unit and want to gain accreditation towards a qualification, first of all you will need to make sure that you are registered with an awarding organisation who offers the qualification. Then you will need to provide a portfolio of evidence for assessment. The person responsible for training within your organisation will advise you about registering with an awarding organisation and give you information about the type of evidence you will need to provide for assessment. You can also get additional information from BILD. For more information about qualifications and assessment please go to the BILD website www.bild.org.uk/qualifications

How this book is organised

Generally each chapter covers one learning outcome from the qualification unit, and one of the Common Induction Standards. The learning outcomes covered are clearly highlighted at the beginning of each chapter. Each chapter starts with a story from a person with a learning disability or family carer or worker. This introduces the topic and is intended to help you think about the topic from their point of view. Each chapter contains:

 Thinking points – to help you reflect on your practice;

Stories – examples of good support from people with learning disabilities and family carers;

 Activities – for you to use to help you to think about your work with people with learning disabilities;

Key points – a summary of the main messages in that chapter;

References and where to go for more information – useful references to help further study.

At the end of the book there is:

A glossary – explaining specialist language in plain English;

An index – to help you look up a particular topic easily.

Study skills

Studying for a qualification can be very rewarding. However, it can be daunting if you have not studied for a long time, or are wondering how to fit your studies into an already busy life. The BILD website contains lots of advice to help you to study successfully, including information about effective reading, taking notes, organising your time, using the internet for research. For further information, go to www.bild.org.uk/qualifications

Chapter 1
Knowing how to recognise signs of abuse

The tenants were given cold sandwiches out of the fridge and the staff went to the chippy. The staff used the tenants' money, from their box, to pay for it. I was amazed that the staff didn't realise they were doing anything wrong.

Karen Flood, summarising one of the many concerns that were raised in national investigations into abuse and neglect she has been involved in

If they found dust in my wardrobe my clothes would be thrown on the floor.

When we had a bath the staff would whip us with towels in places where bruises wouldn't show.

There was a punishment book. If your name went in the punishment book things would stop, like going out or going home.

When you arrived there you became a non-person, you didn't exist.

My life has changed so much since I left. People think you can forget it, but you can't.

Bill Heron talking about his own experiences of living in an institution in the 1980s

Introduction

The stories above show that there are many different types of abuse. Some are obvious, but others might not be as easy to see. There are also many different reasons why abuse occurs. The inquiry into the abuse of people with learning disabilities in the care of Cornwall Partnership NHS Trust identified that staff simply did not know that the way they were working with people was abusive.

The investigation report says:

> Although staff were aware of the procedure for reporting abuse, they were largely unaware of what constituted abuse. …In addition, little training and the practice of unqualified staff predominantly learning by observing their peers, has meant that practices, some of which were very poor, have become ingrained.
>
> *CSCI and Healthcare Commission, 2006*

Learning outcomes

This chapter looks at:

- what is meant when we use the words 'abuse' and 'neglect' and explains the terms physical abuse, sexual abuse, emotional or psychological abuse, financial abuse, institutional abuse, self-neglect and neglect by others;

- the signs and symptoms associated with these types of abuse;

- factors that may contribute to an individual being more vulnerable to abuse.

This chapter covers:

- Common Induction Standards – Standard 6 – Principles of safeguarding in health and social care: Learning Outcome 1

- Level 2 and level 3 HSC 024 level 2 – Principles of safeguarding and protection: Learning Outcome 1

What is abuse?

In *No Secrets* (Department of Health and Home Office, 2000) abuse is described as 'a violation of an individual's human and civil rights by any other person or persons'.

The Council of Europe have defined abuse in the following way:

> Any act, or failure to act, which results in a significant breach of a vulnerable person's human rights, civil liberties, bodily integrity, dignity or general well being; whether intended or inadvertent; including sexual relationships or financial transactions to which a person has not or cannot validly consent, or which are deliberately exploitative.
>
> *Safeguarding Adults and Children with Disabilities Against Abuse. Council of Europe, 2002*

Anyone can experience abuse. Abuse is very often part of a long-term situation, but it can be a one-off event, for example a person with learning disabilities having money stolen from them by a member of staff on just one occasion. It happens when someone either deliberately or unknowingly causes harm or puts life or rights in danger.

It is important that everyone who supports people with learning disabilities understands how to recognise abuse and neglect, and how to report it so that it can be stopped and prevented from happening again in the future.

Abuse and power

There is almost always a link between abuse and power. Anyone providing support to a person who relies on them for support will be in a position of power. This is not always a bad thing and does not always mean that abuse will happen. However, it is important that learning disability workers think about the amount of power they have and how they use it. Are they using it for the benefit of the people they support (in their best interests) or are they using it for their own benefit, which could be classed as abuse?

Thinking point

Think about a person you support and how much they might rely on you to help them to do things. Do you think this puts you in a position of power?

Recognising that you may be in a position of power is an important starting point. You can then think about whether you are really using your position of power to help and support them, or using this power to make life easier or better for you. Find out whether the person you support has a support plan that says which decisions they will make themselves and which will involve others. Look at the plan and find out who might be involved in making decisions with them.

When thinking about safeguarding and protection of people with a learning disability, there are two important concepts to consider: rights and power. Rights are a framework of laws that protect people from harm and set out what people can say and do. Rights guarantee access to a fair trial and other basic entitlements, such as the right to respect and equality. Power means the ability of a person or group of people to exercise authority over another, and so controlling and influencing others.

Types of abuse

Some things are very easy to identify as abuse. For example, it may be easy to identify that hitting an individual who has a learning disability is physical abuse. However, there are other kinds of abuse which are just as damaging and which you need to be aware of.

Physical abuse

Physical abuse includes harming someone by the use of force, or applying inappropriate physical force to manage or restrain a person. Your organisation may have a policy which covers behaviour support, the use of physical interventions or physical restraint of an individual by a suitably qualified person, in certain circumstances. This may state, for example, that restraint is only allowed if all other attempts to manage the behaviour of someone who is acting in a way that is a danger to themselves or to others have failed. If this is the case in your organisation, you will have further information and training during or soon after your induction.

For more information on positive behaviour support, see the *Promote Positive Behaviour* book in this series.

Examples of physical abuse include:

- hitting or kicking someone, pulling their hair or burning them with a cigarette;
- using physical force without a very good reason, which results in physical or psychological harm;
- leaving someone in a situation in which they experience discomfort or pain, such as sitting on the toilet for a long period of time;
- force-feeding someone;
- making someone perform a task for which they don't have the energy or ability;
- leaving someone in an unheated room or outside the building without being properly dressed;
- failing to remove a person from a dangerous situation;
- failing to stop someone being physically abused by another person;
- threatening violence to get people to do things they don't want to do;
- misusing medication to control someone;
- inappropriately restraining someone by tying them to a bed or chair, by any means, so that they are unable to move or react;
- inappropriately locking someone in a room.

Sexual abuse

Sexual abuse is not always obvious. Services need to support the sexuality of the person with a learning disability, and their rights and choices, while at the same time protecting them from abuse. This can be difficult, as circumstances and people vary. Workers supporting people with a learning disability should take care not to prejudge the relationships of those they support, and to ask for advice if they are concerned.

Because of their disability, some people are unable to consent to sexual activity. The Sexual Offences Act 2003 (England and Wales) makes it an offence to take part in sexual activity with anyone who does not have the capacity to consent, and makes clear that consent must be freely given. Courts will assume that consent was not given if a person's disability prevents them from communicating whether they want to have sex or not.

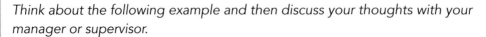

Activity

Think about the following example and then discuss your thoughts with your manager or supervisor.

A young woman with learning disabilities that you support tells you about her new boyfriend that she met at college. She says that he keeps telling her that he wants to be alone with her and that he wants to have sex with her. She says he often touches her and she doesn't like it very much. She is unhappy and asks you for advice.

Discuss what you think you ought to do with your colleagues, and with your supervisor or manager.

Sexual abuse occurs when one person exerts power over another to achieve sexual gratification. It can include a number of actions, including:

- fondling or kissing without consent;
- inappropriate intimate touching of a sexual nature by another person with a learning disability or by others;
- inappropriately or deliberately encouraging sexual arousal 'just for fun';
- encouraging people to talk about their sexual experiences inappropriately;
- making someone do something of a sexual nature against their will;
- engaging in a sexual activity with a person with learning disabilities with whom you have a professional relationship;
- making pornographic material available inappropriately;
- failing to act when you encounter or suspect sexual abuse;
- observing sexually inappropriate activities;
- encouraging sexual relationships between persons with learning disabilities inappropriately;
- taking or sharing sexually explicit photographs or electronic images of an individual with learning disabilities;
- threatening a person with sexual assault or rape.

Note that some of these activities are only considered abusive if they take place between people where there is an imbalance of power. Don't forget that power is used in a variety of different ways, for example by tone of voice, by sarcasm and by the words used. Any sexual contact between a member of staff and a person with learning disabilities is considered abusive.

Emotional and psychological abuse

Emotional or psychological abuse means acting towards someone in a manner that:

- makes them fearful, upset or unhappy;
- causes them a lot of stress or anxiety;
- causes them to act against their will as a result of fear or anxiety.

Examples of emotional or psychological abuse include the following.

Emotional or psychological abuse means acting toward someone in a way that makes them fearful, upset or unhappy or causes them a lot of stress or anxiety

- Bullying – negative, aggressive and targeted behaviour carried out over a period of time. Bullying can be by a support worker, another person with a learning disability, a family member or someone whom the individual encounters in the community such as a member of the public.
- Threats or threatening language.
- Veiled threats, such as 'If you don't do as I say I don't think your Mum will visit you this weekend.'
- Swearing and shouting.
- Having no choice about living with someone who is aggressive or threatening.
- Deliberately discussing experiences that make people feel bad about themselves.
- Reminding people of all the things they are unable to do.
- Deliberately doing things that will 'wind people up'.
- Ignoring people for long periods of time.
- Denying someone's requests, choices, opinions and privacy.
- Restricting access to friends and family.
- Ignoring religious or cultural needs.

Financial abuse

Financial abuse means getting money or property by deception or using other people's money or property against their wishes or the wishes of those looking after their interests.

Financial abuse includes:

- theft of money or belongings from a person with learning disabilities or their family if you are working in their home;

- using money intended for one purpose for a totally different purpose without the free consent of the person concerned;

- asking for money for things which ought to be provided as part of the service;

Financial abuse includes asking for money for things which ought to be provided as part of the service

- borrowing money from a person with learning disabilities (except in real emergencies, when it should be paid back promptly and correctly documented);

- encouraging people to spend money when they don't want to – for example, accusing them of being 'mean';

- placing pressure on the individual to 'buy' their time or friendship;

- pressurising or deceiving people into financial transactions such as changing wills and buying inappropriate goods;

- sharing one person's money with others without their agreement;

- taking advantage of 'offers' when out shopping with a person you support, for example taking home for personal use the 'free' item from a 'buy one get one free' promotion or adding points to a personal store loyalty card without the consent of the person you are supporting.

It is important to remember that financial abuse can also include misusing people's property or their family's property. For example, a member of staff using a phone belonging to someone they support, to make their own personal phone calls, or a member of staff eating or drinking food which belongs to the person they are supporting.

Over the last few years, in England and Wales, there have been a growing number of cases reported involving a misuse of Powers of Attorney. For example, someone might have appointed a relative with Lasting Power of Attorney when they were initially diagnosed with dementia, so that this relative could manage their money when they became unable to do this for themselves. The

Financial abuse can include abuse of property such as a staff member using the phone of someone they support to make personal phone calls

person's dementia has now got worse and the family member is managing their money for them, but is using some of this for their own benefit, rather than for the benefit of the vulnerable adult.

Institutional abuse

Institutional abuse is abuse which has become commonplace in a service and which restricts the freedom of people, harms them or denies their human rights. This sort of abuse usually arises when the smooth running of the service or the needs of the staff are put before the needs of the person with learning disabilities they are there to support. It also takes place where bad work practices have become the norm and nobody seems to question them. There may be a lack of individual support for the people using the service, for example where everyone has the same mealtimes, bedtimes, dresses in similar ways and has similar haircuts.

Thinking point

If you work in an organisation such as a residential home or day service, think about an average day and the usual routines. Are all of these for the benefit of the people you support, or are some of them there to make the running of the service easier, or because 'this is the way things are done here'? How much involvement do the people you support and family carers have in deciding how things are done within the service?

Institutional abuse may include things such as:

- having strict rules by which people are controlled, like being allowed out only with permission;

- people having their bags, rooms or person searched;

- being prevented from doing things which are their right;

- having their mail read;

- going into people's rooms without their permission;

- leaving the bathroom door open;

- giving medicine to control behaviour so that an individual does not disrupt the smooth running of the service, rather than for valid medical reasons;

- having to share clothing with other people.

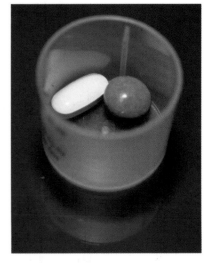

Giving medication to manage behaviour so an individual doesn't disrupt the smooth running of the service, rather than for valid medical reasons, may be institutional abuse

Neglect by others

Neglect means systematically and consistently failing to respond to a person's needs or failing to take actions in their best interests. It can be deliberate, but is not always done on purpose. For example, people in the person's life failing to check out or anticipate the individual's wishes or needs.

In certain cases neglect can also be classed as a criminal offence. The Mental Capacity Act 2005 (in England and Wales) introduced the offence of 'wilful neglect'. This means that if someone in a caring role neglects the needs of someone who lacks mental capacity, they could face criminal charges. The maximum sentence for wilful neglect is up to five years' imprisonment and a fine of up to £2000.

Examples of neglect include:

- paid workers not passing on essential information to family carers where this will put a person with a learning disability at risk, or vice versa;

- leaving someone in bed all day in a residential home because there are staff shortages;

- failing to support someone in an activity outside their home because the member of staff doesn't enjoy the activity or doesn't feel like going;

- not getting medical attention for someone who is ill;

- exposing people to unreasonable risk, such as allowing them to ride in a car without wearing a seat belt;

- allowing a person to put on excessive weight without discussing risks and possible strategies with all care partners;

- not removing a person from threats from someone with challenging behaviours;

- failing to ensure that people are well equipped for, capable of and suited to any activity which is potentially harmful, such as some sports;

- allowing someone to travel on public transport alone, when the possible risks have not been identified;

- failing to stop someone going off with a person who could harm them;

- failing to follow the risk assessment for an individual you support.

Self neglect

Self neglect takes different forms. We are all guilty of it at times, for instance when we neglect our health needs or don't get enough sleep.

Thinking point

Do you ever stay out until the early hours of the morning and get up to go to work a few hours later? Do you feel that you have a healthy diet all the time or are there times when you eat a lot of junk food? Would you ever consider these things to be self neglect?

When self neglect becomes dangerous, we have a duty to do something about it. The kind of self neglect we are talking about could be when someone:

- puts themselves at risk through not taking essential medication, for example for epileptic seizures;

- fails to take enough care of their health or to deal with a potentially harmful illness or injury;

- drinks alcohol when taking medication that reacts badly with it;

- doesn't wear their glasses or hearing aid when they need to;

- takes risks with safety, like trying something dangerous without adequate safeguards or support, or going out alone after dark to places known to be dangerous.

There are other commonplace situations which, if taken to extreme, could amount to self neglect. These include:

- someone keeping the house in a very dirty state so that it is a health hazard;

- someone not wearing the right clothes for bad weather;

- staying in bed for a number of days and not eating;

- someone not washing for long periods, so their health could be affected and other people choose to stay away from them.

Much of this will depend on the person's ability and understanding of the risks involved. It is essential to recognise people's right to run their lives as they wish and to respect their privacy. However, if the situation is extreme and there is a danger to the person concerned, the support worker has a duty to act. This should always be done by talking with the person, unless this is not possible, for instance if the person is gravely ill or extremely depressed and cannot take part in decision-making. When the self neglect also puts others at risk there may be a need to act even if the person concerned is unwilling to agree.

One of the main principles of the Mental Capacity Act 2005 is that a person should not be treated as unable to make a decision just because their decision may seem unwise. This means that the people you support have the right to make decisions that other people might not agree with, as long as they fully understand what might happen as a result. However, you still have a duty of care to make sure that the person has all the information they need to make an informed decision. It is also important that any potential risks have been assessed and measures put in place to minimise these risks. It is good practice to include relatives in this – they may have valuable information to contribute and will want to know how support decisions are made.

There may also be situations where self neglect is the result of a lack of support or where the person simply cannot manage what is expected of them. In such situations it is neglect by others that is the main problem.

Other types of abuse

It is important to remember that people with learning disabilities may also be the victims of abuse on the grounds of race, gender or sexual orientation, age or disability. These types of abuse happen because of prejudice and discrimination towards minority groups in society, not only towards people with disabilities. The term that is generally used is 'discriminatory abuse' and this might be included as a form of abuse in your local safeguarding policies.

Valuing People Now: A new three year strategy for learning disabilities (Department of Health, 2009), which covers England, has identified a number of groups of people with learning disabilities that tend to face increased exclusion and discrimination.

- People with more complex needs (including people with profound and multiple learning disabilities and people whose behaviour presents a challenge).

- People from black and minority ethnic groups and newly arrived communities.

- People on the autistic spectrum.

- Offenders in custody and the community.

The book *Equality and Inclusion for Learning Disability Workers* in this series covers the topic of discrimination in more detail.

Recognising the signs and symptoms of abuse and neglect

It is essential that you, as a learning disability worker, are aware of the signs and indicators of abuse so that you can report it, prevent it happening and play your part in helping people to deal with it. However, you should be aware that just because you have identified some signs and symptoms of abuse, it does not mean that abuse is definitely taking place. There may be another explanation – so take care not to jump to conclusions.

It is important that you report all concerns you have about people you support even if you are unsure whether or not abuse might be involved

It is important that you report all concerns you have about the people you support, to a line manager or supervisor, even if you are unsure whether or not abuse might be involved. For example, you might be supporting someone who does not communicate verbally and you notice that there have been some changes in the person's behaviour. This could potentially be a sign of abuse, but could also indicate that the person is worried, upset, in pain, or that something else is wrong. The important thing is that you report it, so that people can look into the reasons for the changes and then take proper steps to address them.

Signs and indicators of physical abuse

Some of the signs of abuse are common to several types of abuse; others are more specific. Some of the common signs and indicators of physical abuse are:

- telling someone that they have been physically abused;
- flinching or shying away from physical contact;
- showing aggression towards other people;
- not wanting to have any medical attention;
- wearing long sleeves, collars or scarves (to cover bruising) even in very hot weather;
- not wanting to take part in activities that involve undressing, such as: swimming or sports activities, especially if the person usually enjoys these;
- being absent from a service or activity regularly with no real explanation;
- repeatedly having unexplained bruises, cuts, burns, scalds or bites;
- explaining away injuries by saying that they fell or bumped into something;
- being afraid of going home or to a place where abuse is happening;
- showing fear of a particular individual.

Signs and indicators of sexual abuse

Some of the common signs and indicators of sexual abuse are:

- telling someone that they have been sexually abused;
- unexplained discharges or bleeding;
- bruising in private areas of the body (such as top of the legs);
- sudden unexplained changes in behaviour;
- sudden and frequent mood swings;
- becoming very withdrawn;
- starting to behave in a much more sexual way than usual for that person;
- standing too close and behaving in inappropriate ways with friends or support workers;
- making inappropriate sexual advances to other people;
- having much greater difficulty in concentrating than before;
- becoming easily sexually aroused, sometimes for no obvious reason;
- becoming very excitable;
- becoming preoccupied by sex;
- starting to tell you things about sex or ask you questions in a roundabout way, saying they have something private to tell you, but seeming unable to talk about it;
- receiving gifts and being unable or unwilling to explain why they have been given;
- obsessive behaviour, such as washing compulsively;
- not wanting to have help with personal care, which is unusual for the person;
- self-harming, for example cutting themselves;
- raising concerns about their own sexuality.

There are other indicators of sexual abuse shown, not by the person being abused, but by the abuser, who could be a colleague, another individual who uses the service, a family member or a friend. These include:

- a worker showing an inappropriate interest in someone who uses the service;
- someone being secretive about their activities with a person;

- finding someone in a compromising situation with an individual and trying to explain it away;

- a worker sexually harassing someone who uses the service by inappropriate touching or suggestive comments;

- a worker who seems to spend a great deal of time with a particular person or group of people inappropriately;

- a worker who develops a close relationship with a person who uses the service which appears to cross professional boundaries.

It is important to remember that the indicators mentioned above might happen for other reasons. They don't necessarily mean that abuse is occurring. However, sudden changes in the way someone acts and extremes of behaviour should always alert you to the possibility that something is wrong.

Signs and indicators of emotional abuse

Some of the common signs and indicators of emotional abuse are:

- becoming increasingly withdrawn;

- being afraid to say anything for fear of ridicule;

- speaking very quietly or in a whisper, sometimes covering their mouth as they speak;

- making fun of themselves, but in an excited way, looking for reactions;

- appearing to have no emotional reactions to anything;

- always shunning company;

- constantly seeking reassurance;

- being moody and unhappy;

- finding it very difficult to get along with other people;

- constantly arguing and challenging other people;

- disturbed sleep patterns;

- changes in eating patterns, for example 'going off' food or 'comfort eating'.

A person who emotionally abuses others may:

- shout a lot and use bullying behaviour;

- threaten people and try to control their behaviour to make them do what they want;

- constantly make fun of people and say nasty things about them;

- take delight in making people afraid or making them cry;

- find it difficult to relate to people – colleagues as well as the people they support.

It is also important to remember that abusers may not appear to be any different from anybody else and may indeed appear to be charming. This is one reason why abusers are sometimes able to carry out abuse over a long period of time.

Thinking point

What is the difference between informing someone of the consequences of their actions and threatening someone? You may have to inform a person you support of the consequences of their actions, but you need to do this in a way that doesn't turn into a threat. For example, you might be due to support someone to go out shopping, but because of their current behaviour (shouting at other people in the house, throwing items about and slapping themselves) you feel it would be best to delay this until the person has calmed down. You will have to explain to the person the effects of their behaviour on other people if they were to go out at the moment, but in a way that still respected the person's rights.

Signs and indicators of financial abuse

Many individuals who have learning disabilities need support with managing their money. People who financially abuse may be deliberately taking advantage of such individuals, or may not realise that what they are doing is financial abuse. When a person is being financially abused you may see one or more of these signs or indicators:

- money disappearing without explanation;

- someone suddenly getting money without explanation;

- lack of transparency about the way money is used – some people being 'in the know' about finances and others left uninformed, for example;

- large surpluses building up but services being cut or of poor quality or equipment being in a poor state;

- a person's money being spent without their involvement;

- the person buying items which are out of character;

- property going missing without trace;

- a change in appearance, for example someone looking scruffy when they previously had been smartly dressed;
- a lack of food or heating.

Signs and indicators of institutional abuse

An investigation into services for people with learning disabilities provided by a primary care trust in England in 2006 found that institutional abuse was common in most parts of the service. The lifestyles and needs of the individuals were sacrificed in favour of the needs of the service. The Healthcare Commission report of January 2007 said, 'This type of institutional abuse was largely unintentional, but it is abuse nevertheless'.

When abusive practices become the norm in an organisation you may find some or all of these signs and indicators:

- staff needs and wishes being put first and the wishes and choices of the people they support not being followed up;
- a service being run in a regimented fashion;
- no opportunity for people who use the service to take part in choices or decision-making;
- no recognition of cultural or religious diversity;
- self-advocacy groups being forbidden or discouraged;
- family members and carers being made unwelcome;
- people's needs, such as special diets or particular medical needs, being ignored;
- punishment being part of the regime;
- physical restraint being regularly used as a means of control with no reference to a person's support plan and without using ways to defuse and manage situations;
- an atmosphere of fear in the service and a sense that people have given up;
- being charged for things, such as transport, that should be provided as part of the service.

Signs and indicators of neglect

Sometimes it is easy to tell if someone is being abused through neglect, but sometimes the signs are quite subtle. Some of the things which should alert you to the possibility of neglect are:

- a person being absent on a regular basis from their work, day service or college for reasons that you suspect are not genuine;

- people from the same residential service wearing one another's clothes regularly;

- a person dressing inadequately for the weather or in ill-fitting or very old clothes while others in their family with whom they live are better dressed;

- someone who lives in the family home seeming to do all the chores in the house or being kept at home regularly in order to look after other family members, regardless of their own needs or wishes;

- family repeatedly stopping their relative from joining in extra activities or outings, giving no clear reason;

- an individual never seeming to have any money although you know they receive disability allowances or get a wage from work;

- an individual not having proper access to health care, social care or educational activities;

- the staff who support the individual not seeming to know much about the individual and being unable to provide the support they need.

It can be very difficult to prove abuse through neglect, particularly in the family home. Every family organises life in a way that suits them. Apparent lack of money may just reflect a parent being overcautious or not recognising the adult status of their son or daughter. This needs to be tackled, but is not neglect. In fact, it is usually quite the opposite and is sometimes called 'overprotectiveness'. If you suspect that this is happening to someone you support, you should not tackle it yourself, but inform your line manager, who should be able to take action.

You should now be able to discuss why it is important to recognise the signs and symptoms of abuse and neglect and relate this to your everyday work supporting people with learning disabilities.

Activity

Think about the people you support and the ways in which they communicate. How would you pick up on possible signs of these people being abused? For example, some of the people you support might not be able to tell you verbally what has happened. Make a list of possible signs and indicators of the different forms of abuse that you think you might pick up on in your particular area of work, and then discuss these with your supervisor or manager.

What makes people with learning disabilities vulnerable to abuse and neglect

There are some groups of people who are more vulnerable to abuse than others. They are known as 'vulnerable adults'.

Vulnerable adults

A broad definition of 'vulnerable adult' taken from the government report *No Secrets: Guidance on developing and implementing multi-agency policies and procedures to protect vulnerable adults from abuse* (section 2, page 8) is:

> a person who is or may be in need of community care services by reason of mental or other disability, age or illness; and who is or may be unable to take care of him or herself, or unable to protect him or herself against significant harm or exploitation.

No Secrets

You can see from this that 'vulnerable adults' can include older people who are physically or mentally frail, people who are physically disabled, people with mental health needs, as well as people with learning disabilities. However, there are a number of reasons why people with learning disabilities may be particularly vulnerable to abuse.

The more dependent someone is on others for support, the less control they have over their lives, and the more vulnerable to abuse they become		
Independence		Dependence
Control		Lack of control
Power		Lack of power

Increasing vulnerability

Reasons for vulnerability to abuse

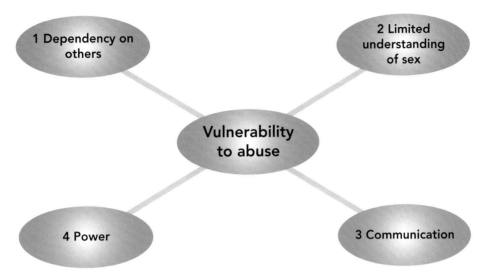

1 Dependency on others

- Some people with learning disabilities are, to a greater or lesser extent, dependent on others, for example for personal care or to help manage their finances. The more dependent a person is, the more vulnerable they are.
- There is more opportunity to abuse someone who needs help with intimate personal care needs.
- In many 'care' situations, it is easy for an abuser to spend time alone with individuals with learning disabilities.
- People may have limited experience with money and may not be confident with budgeting and handling money, so they are more likely to need support with financial matters.

2 Limited understanding about sex and relationships

- Some people have a limited understanding about sex and so they can't consent to it. They may not understand that sex is different from other things such as having support with personal care, for example help to go to the toilet or bathing.
- Because of their level of ability and understanding, as well as limited experience, some people may not understand the difference between friendship, a legitimate sexual relationship and sexual abuse.
- The sexual identity of people with learning disabilities is often ignored. People wishing to explore their sexuality may agree to the relationship even if it is an abusive one – they may not understand the notion of abuse.

3 Communication

- Some people may have difficulty with verbal communication and may be unable to report what is happening, or to say 'no' to the abuser.

- People may not know how to complain about how they are being treated, or other people may not take the complaint seriously or even believe it.

- People feel they won't be listened to if they do speak up.

4 Power

- Abusers are often people who have some authority over the person being abused. It is difficult for the abused person to speak out against them because they may be frightened, don't know who to tell or think nothing can be done.

- The abuser may have threatened the person, who may fear that the abuser will carry out their threat if they speak out.

- Many people with learning disabilities have few friends. They may be pleased about receiving attention from someone they like and respect and not realise that they are being abused.

Settings where abuse may take place

Abuse can take place anywhere – in a person's own home, within a residential home or a day care establishment or in a public place. Some forms of abuse are more likely to happen in certain situations than in others, for example:

- where a service or individual is isolated and where people have limited contact with their local community and family, then neglect such as poor conditions and not giving appropriate medication can happen;

- people who have difficulty in communicating verbally or people with multiple disabilities are at greater risk of being abused physically, financially and sexually.

Thinking point

A lot of people with learning disabilities are now receiving direct payments or individual budgets, which help them to have more choice and control over their support. Having greater independence and control should lead to people being less vulnerable to abuse. However, some people have argued that if less monitoring and regulation of support are provided through direct payments and individual budgets, this could result in some people with learning disabilities being more vulnerable to abuse.

Do you support anyone who receives a direct payment or individual budget? If so, what steps have been taken to identify and prevent possible abuse?

Activity

Think about a typical day of someone you support. Make a list of the places the person spends time in that day and note whether the person might be more vulnerable to abuse in some of those settings than in others. Identify the forms of abuse which may be more likely to occur in each of the settings you have identified.

People who abuse

There is a wide range of people who may abuse a person with learning disabilities, including:

- staff working with people with learning disabilities such as day or residential staff, leisure centre workers or colleagues in work placement settings;
- close family members or more distant relatives;
- friends and neighbours;
- a partner;
- a volunteer;
- work colleagues of people with learning disabilities;
- people in other positions of authority, such as religious leaders, youth workers or club leaders;

- other people with learning or other disabilities;

- strangers or people who see the person regularly so are familiar to them, but are possibly not known to the family or staff.

It is more likely that an abuser is known to the individual with learning disabilities. In all cases abuse occurs because there is an unequal power relationship between the person with a learning disability and the abuser.

As mentioned above, people with learning disabilities can abuse other people with learning disabilities. The abuse might not always be intentional – sometimes the person being abusive doesn't realise that what they are doing is a form of abuse. However, abuse is mainly related to the impact on the alleged victim and not on the intentions of the alleged abuser. For example, two people with learning disabilities might live in the same supported-living tenancy, and one regularly bullies the other into doing all the cooking, washing up and housework, because they don't like doing this. The person doing the bullying uses threats of physical violence ('I'll hit you if you don't wash up now'), calls the other person nasty names and says 'you're stupid – no one will listen to you'. This involves a misuse of power and should still be dealt with through safeguarding procedures. You would need to report the situation to your line manager and make a record of everything you had seen and heard.

Key points from this chapter

- There are a number of different forms of abuse, but all of them involve a violation of someone's human and civil rights.

- Abuse involves a misuse of power – usually when power is used in a negative and controlling way.

- Some people abuse others on purpose, but in many cases the abuser did not intend to harm the other person.

- Many people with learning disabilities have little power in society.

- People with learning disabilities may be vulnerable for a number of reasons. Vulnerability is linked to dependence, lack of control and power.

- Anyone can be an abuser, but it is more likely that they are known to the person with learning disabilities.

- It is important to be able to recognise abuse and neglect so that it can be stopped, and so that bad practices among some staff are not passed on to other workers.

- You must report all concerns, even if you are unsure whether it is abuse or not, so it can be looked into.

- Everyone who supports people with learning disabilities should be able to recognise the signs and indicators of abuse and neglect so that they can report it and play a part in getting it stopped.

- Although there are some settings where some types of abuse are more likely to occur, abuse can take place anywhere, in any situation.

References and where to go for more information

References

Council of Europe (2002) *Safeguarding Adults and Children with Disabilities Against Abuse.* Strasbourg: Council of Europe Publishing

Legislation, policies and reports

All UK legislation can be downloaded from www.legislation.gov.uk Policies and reports for Northern Ireland, Scotland and Wales can be found at www.northernireland.gov.uk www.scotland.gov.uk and www.wales.gov.uk respectively. Policies and reports for England can be found on the website of the relevant government department.

Adult Support and Protection (Scotland) Act 2007

Sexual Offences Act 2003

Department of Health (2009) *Valuing People Now: A new three year strategy for learning disabilities.* London: Department of Health

Department of Health and Home Office (2000) *No Secrets: Guidance on developing and implementing multi-agency policies and procedures to protect vulnerable adults from abuse.* London: Department of Health (covers England)

Department of Health, Social Services and Public Safety (2010) *Adult Safeguarding in Northern Ireland, Regional and Local Partnership Arrangements.* Belfast: Department of Health, Social Services and Public Safety (covers Northern Ireland)

Lord Chancellor's Department (1997) *Who Decides? Making decisions on behalf of mentally incapacitated adults: a consultation paper presented to parliament.* Quoted in Department of Health and Home Office (2000)

Office of the Public Guardian (2007) *Mental Capacity Act (2005) Code of Practice.* London: The Stationery Office

Scottish Care Commission (2008) *Adult Support and Protection Policy & Procedure.* Dundee: Scottish Commission for the Regulation of Care

Welsh Assembly (2000) *In Safe Hands: Implementing adult protection procedures in Wales.* Cardiff: Welsh Assembly Government

Chapter 2

Understanding the national and local context of safeguarding and protection from abuse

We want people to be safe in our area, but as a result of reviewing our local multi-agency safeguarding procedures we realised that they were difficult to follow. Also there was too much jargon, responsibilities were unclear, timescales were unrealistic and some roles were inappropriate. This had led to pockets of poor practice and poor experiences for people in the borough.

So, we decided to carry out extensive consultation with the people who were supposed to have responsibility under the procedures to make them workable, robust and realistic.

This led to the production of new multi-agency Safeguarding Policy, Procedures and Good Practice Guidance in 2010. The process – roles, responsibilities, and timescales – are now much clearer, and the procedures are easier for everyone to follow.

We want people to feel confident using our local safeguarding policies whether they are people with disabilities, family carers or workers.

Service manager adult safeguarding, English local authority, 2010

Introduction

It can be hard to believe that someone who is employed to support a person with a learning disability might harm them but, sadly, this does happen. Sometimes people target vulnerable adults on purpose to exploit or harm them, but more often it is because the worker lacks knowledge, understanding or skills. The government has put in place national policies and procedures to safeguard vulnerable adults. These form the basis of the policies and procedures relating to abuse which are put in place by the organisation you work for. If you are a personal assistant employed by the person you support, you are also covered by the national legislation and the local policies.

Policies and procedure

A policy is a statement of the approach that will be taken regarding particular issues. There are key national policies relating to abuse. Your organisation will also have policies relating to abuse and these will be based on the national guidelines.

A procedure is a set of instructions on how the policy should be put into practice. Your organisation's procedures relating to the safeguarding of vulnerable adults will relate directly to the policy.

If you work as a personal assistant, your employer, the person you support, may have policies and procedures relating to abuse and you should follow these. However, if they do not have policies and procedures for you to follow you are still bound by the national legislation and you should make yourself aware of the local adult safeguarding policies by contacting your local authority.

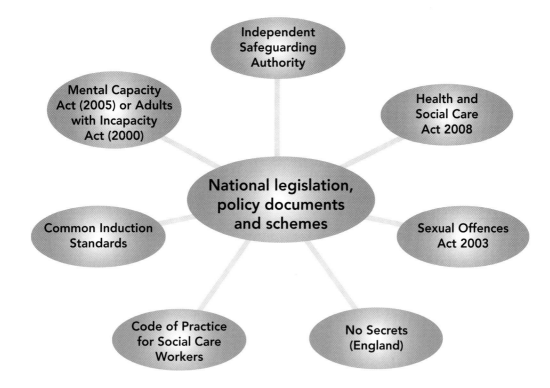

National legislation, policy documents, schemes and reports.

Key national legislation

Although many laws include safeguards for vulnerable adults, there are three Acts of Parliament that are particularly relevant.

Health and Social Care Act 2008

This Act led to the setting up of the Care Quality Commission, which is responsible for inspecting and regulating health, social care and mental health services in England. From 1 October 2010 every health and social care service in England is legally responsible for making sure it meets new essential standards of quality and safety. Outcome 7 of the standards is 'Safeguarding people who use services from abuse'. The Care Quality Commission is the regulator of health and social care services in England. There are separate regulators for Wales, Scotland and Northern Ireland listed in the reference section at the end of this chapter.

Sexual Offences Act 2003

This Act, which applies in England and Wales, changed the law on rape and sexual assault so that offences covered sexual activity with someone who does not have the capacity to consent. The term 'mental disorder' is used in the Act to cover individuals with learning disabilities.

The legislation in Scotland is the Sexual Offences (Scotland) Act 2009, and in Northern Ireland the legislation is the Sexual Offences (Northern Ireland) Order 2008.

New offences were created including:

- offences against persons with a mental disorder who are unable to consent;

- inducements, threats and deceptions to persons with a mental disorder.

The offences apply to workers caring for people with a mental disorder and strengthen the law as it assumes that support workers understand better than others that the individual could not consent.

Mental Capacity Act 2005

The Act came into force in England and Wales in 2007 and it sets out what should happen when someone lacks capacity to make choices and decisions. The five principles are as follows.

- All adults are assumed to have the capacity to make choices and decisions, unless proved otherwise.

- Everyone should be given all the support and help that they need to make a decision before anyone concludes that they lack capacity.

- People cannot be assessed as lacking capacity purely on the basis of their making unwise decisions.

- Any actions taken or decisions made on behalf of someone who lacks capacity must be done in their best interests.

- Any decisions made must be those that have the least restrictions on a person's freedom and rights.

The Act introduced the new criminal offence of ill-treatment or wilful neglect of a person who lacks capacity. If convicted, people can be imprisoned or fined. This covers a failure to provide adequate care, restraining someone unreasonably against their will and any type of abuse or neglect.

There is different legislation in Scotland and Northern Ireland (see the References section for details).

Independent Mental Capacity Advocates

The Mental Capacity Act 2005 introduced the role of the Independent Mental Capacity Advocate (IMCA) service in England and Wales. The purpose of the IMCA service is to help vulnerable people who lack capacity to make important decisions about serious medical treatment and changes of accommodation, and who have no family or friends that it would be appropriate to consult about those decisions. The role of the IMCA is to work with and support people who lack capacity, and represent their views to those who are working to determine their best interests. IMCAs can also work with people who lack capacity in care reviews and safeguarding adults cases (even if family are involved).

Deprivation of Liberty Safeguards (DOLS)

The Mental Capacity Act 2005 has been amended to provide safeguards for people who lack capacity specifically to consent to treatment or care in either a hospital or care home that, in their own best interests, can only be provided in circumstances that amount to a deprivation of liberty. This might involve stopping someone from doing something they want to do, because they do not understand the risks involved. A number of assessments have to be carried out to make sure that the person does lack capacity to make the decision, that the decision is in the person's best interests and that a lawful process has been followed.

Key national policy documents

These policy documents contain national guidelines about safeguarding vulnerable adults. They should inform your organisation's policies on abuse.

No Secrets: Guidance on developing and implementing multi-agency policies and procedures to protect vulnerable adults from abuse

'It is important for all organisations in England that might come into contact with vulnerable adults in a local area to work together to develop common policies and procedures' (Department of Health, 2000). Organisations which should work together include:

- local authority adult social services departments;

- all NHS services in the area;

- organisations which provide residential care for vulnerable adults;

- organisations providing domiciliary care;

- inspectors of services, such as the Care Quality Commission (CQC);

- benefits agencies;

- other local authority departments such as housing;

- police;

- probation services;

- carers' support groups;

- groups of people who use services.

The local authority social services department co-ordinates all of this work and produces safeguarding adults procedures for the area. You should have a copy in your organisation. If not, you should be able to obtain a copy from your local social services department or download it from your local authority's website. Your organisation will need to follow the safeguarding adults procedures for your area in their own policies and procedures.

In many areas there is now a multi-agency Safeguarding Adults Board (made up of representatives from a wide range of organisations), which co-ordinates the implementation of the multi-agency safeguarding adults policy and procedures.

The *No Secrets* guidance relates specifically to England. The documents for Scotland, Northern Ireland and Wales are listed in the reference section at the end of this chapter.

No Secrets was reviewed throughout 2008/2009 and the results of this review can be found on the Department of Health website.

Safeguarding adults

This report, published by the Association of Directors of Social Services in 2005, brings together all the good practice which has been developed in adult protection since *No Secrets* and offers a national framework of standards for good practice and outcomes in adult protection work.

Code of Practice for Social Care Workers

The code states that as a social care worker you must 'respect the rights of service users while protecting them as far as possible from danger or harm' (General Social Care Council, September 2002; this covers England only, and details of the other three national councils are at the end of this chapter). In addition, the General Social Care Council is the organisation in England with responsibility for the professional registration of all social workers. Anyone registered with GSCC who has been found guilty of abuse or neglect is likely to be struck off and be unable to work in social care in the future. Details about the equivalent bodies to the GSCC and the Codes of Practice in the other countries of the UK are available from the Northern Ireland Social Care Council, the Scottish Social Services Council and the Care Council for Wales.

Common Induction Standards

These are the national standards which the induction of all new care workers should follow (Skills for Care, 2010; England only). The induction that you undertake as a new worker specifically includes information about abuse and neglect. This is because it is an important topic that all workers in social care should know about. Your organisation has a responsibility to induct all of its new staff and to include training on abuse and neglect.

Valuing People Now: A new three year strategy for learning disabilities

One of the policy objectives within *Valuing People Now* is: 'People with learning disabilities will be able to lead their lives in safe environments and will feel confident that their right to live in safety is upheld by the criminal justice system' (Department of Health, January 2009).

Key National Scheme

The Vetting and Barring Scheme

The Vetting and Barring Scheme is one of the government's key responses to the Soham murders (involving Ian Huntley). The inquiry which followed these murders, known as the Bichard Inquiry, recommended a new scheme that would ensure that everyone working in regulated activity with children or vulnerable adults is checked and registered. The inquiry led to the Safeguarding Vulnerable Groups Act 2006 and the Safeguarding Vulnerable Groups (Northern Ireland) Order 2007, which provide for the establishment of the scheme in England, Wales and Northern Ireland. There are separate arrangements and legislation in Scotland. In Scotland the government introduced in 2011 a new membership scheme to replace and improve upon the current disclosure arrangements for people who work with vulnerable groups.The Protecting Vulnerable Groups Scheme (PVG Scheme) delivers on the provisions outlined in the Protection of Vulnerable Groups (PVG) (Scotland) Act 2007.

The Independent Safeguarding Authority (ISA) has been set up to make decisions about who should be barred from working with vulnerable groups. Instead of having several different lists of barred individuals (which had been the case), the ISA maintains a single list of people barred from working with children and a single list relating to vulnerable adults.

The scheme began in October 2009 with the implementation of the ISA's new barred lists (replacing, for example, the Protection of Vulnerable Adults Scheme). When people apply to work (in either a paid or voluntary capacity) with children or vulnerable adults, they are checked against the ISA lists (in addition to the usual Criminal Record Bureau check). If a member of staff or volunteer is found guilty of abuse they can be referred to the ISA, who will then decide if the person should be barred from working with vulnerable groups.

There was also a plan that people working with children and vulnerable adults (either paid or voluntary) would have to register with the ISA, with the registration scheme starting in July 2010. However, the government is currently reviewing the criminal records and vetting and barring systems and has put this registration on hold until the review has been completed.

Reports into serious failures to protect vulnerable adults

The joint investigation into the provision of services for people with learning disabilities at Cornwall Partnership NHS Trust

This investigation was started because of serious concerns raised by family carers from East Cornwall Mencap Society about the care and treatment of people supported by the Trust (CSCI/Healthcare Commission, July 2006). An investigation was carried out by the Healthcare Commission and the Commission for Social Care Inspection. It found that there were significant failings in the quality and safety of care being provided by the Trust for people with learning disabilities. A number of cases of abuse were highlighted. The report concluded that the welfare of some people was at risk and that urgent action was needed to ensure their safety. A number of recommendations were made about changes in the way services were delivered. This inquiry has important lessons for everyone who supports people with learning disabilities.

Investigation into the service for people with learning disabilities provided by the Sutton and Merton Primary Care Trust

This investigation took place because the chief executive of Sutton and Merton Primary Care Trust had requested an independent investigation following a number of serious incidents in learning disability services, including allegations of physical and sexual abuse (Healthcare Commission, January 2007). There were some similarities between the findings in this investigation and the investigation into Cornwall Partnership NHS Trust. One of these was that institutional abuse was widespread but that staff were unaware that what they were doing was actually abuse. As with the Cornwall investigation, changes were suggested into the way services are delivered.

As a result of the Cornwall investigation the Healthcare Commission decided to carry out an inspection of all learning disability services run by the NHS in England.

Serious case review into the murder of Steven Hoskin

Steven Hoskin, a 39-year-old man with learning disabilities, was murdered in 2006 by a group of people who had targeted him because he was vulnerable. The serious case review described how a number of different agencies had been in regular contact with Steven, but none of these recognised how much danger he was in, and each agency failed to share information with the other organisations involved (Cornwall Adult Protection Committee, December 2007). The following information is taken from the serious case review executive summary:

> All agencies have legal responsibilities not only to prevent harm being caused by their own agents, but to safeguard vulnerable people against the harmful actions of third parties. What is striking about the responses of services to Steven's circumstances is that each agency focused on single issues within their own sectional remits and did not make the connections deemed necessary for the protection of vulnerable adults and proposed by *No Secrets*.
>
> *The Stephen Hoskin serious case review (2007)* www.cornwall.gov.uk

Your organisation's policies about abuse and neglect

All organisations should have policies and procedures that help workers to recognise and respond to abuse and neglect. All workers should know where these policies and procedures can be found and what they say. The families of the individuals you support should also know about these policies so that they can be confident that the service will do all it possibly can to protect their relative. People who use the service should have an accessible copy.

Activity

Find and read through your organisation's policy and procedure on abuse and neglect. If there is anything you are unclear about, ask your line manager. Make notes on the following questions.

- *How does your organisation define abuse?*
- *What steps does your organisation say you should take if you discover or suspect abuse?*
- *Whom should you go to for guidance if you need to discuss an abusive or potentially abusive situation?*
- *What should relatives do if they suspect abuse?*

If your organisation doesn't have a policy on abuse, this is a very serious matter. You should talk to your manager about this and you may have to report it to your local council social services department or the social care regulator for your country. If you work as a personal assistant, you need to ask your employer about training on abuse and what you should do if you suspect abuse.

Discuss this activity with your line manager or employer at your next supervision.

Your organisation's policy on abuse should be based on the legislation and national policies outlined above and should clearly describe how the organisation will respond to situations of abuse and neglect. Your organisation's procedures should tell workers what they should do if abuse is suspected or when abuse has been disclosed. The procedures should give the worker clear information about what they should do in particular situations.

The policy and procedures in your organisation should include:

- a clear definition of abuse;
- guidance for staff on recognising abuse;
- details of responsibilities when dealing with abuse;
- information on the reporting of abuse and suspected abuse.

Every member of staff should be familiar with these documents. Your organisation should regularly review these policies and procedures in the light of national changes in the law and guidance and in the light of experience in using the policies and procedures.

In addition your organisation has a duty to make sure that the people who use your service:

- know what 'abuse' means;
- recognise when they are in danger of any kind of abuse;
- know what to do and whom to talk to if they are worried about abuse or being abused.

Activity

Protecting vulnerable adults from abuse and neglect is not achieved just by having a safeguarding adults policy and procedure. There will be many other policies and procedures that help in protecting people from abuse and neglect. For example, financial procedures will include things like the need to keep receipts for purchases, not accepting gifts from the people you support, etc. List all the other policies and procedures that you think will help to maintain the safety and wellbeing of the people you support, and then run through this list with your manager or supervisor.

Key points from this chapter

- The government develops national laws and guidance, and the policies and procedures that you use are based on these. Policies and procedures need to be regularly reviewed to make sure they are still up to date with national laws and guidance.

- Within each local authority there is a multi-agency safeguarding adults policy and procedure. This is usually co-ordinated by the local authority adult social services department. Your organisation's policies must link in with the multi-agency policy.

- You need to make sure you have a good working knowledge of the policies and procedures in your own organisation that protect vulnerable adults from abuse and neglect.

- A number of national reports show that abuse is still common within services and that this is often caused by staff not having a good understanding of what abuse actually is. This is why induction and training are so important – so you have a good understanding of what abuse is and what you must do about any concerns of abuse.

- You should make sure that you have read and understood your organisation's policies and procedures relating to abuse and neglect, and that you follow them in your work. If you are a personal assistant, talk to your employer about any policies or agreed ways of working that you should be following.

References and where to go for more information

References

Association of Directors of Social Services (2005) *Safeguarding Adults: A national framework of standards for good practice and outcomes in adult protection work.* London: ADSS

Cornwall Adult Protection Committee (2007) *The Murder of Steven Hoskin, Serious Case Review, Executive Summary* (available at: www.cornwall.gov.uk)

CSCI/Healthcare Commission (2006) *Joint Investigation into the Provision of Services for People with Learning Disabilities at Cornwall Partnership NHS Trust.* London: CSCI and Healthcare Commission

Healthcare Commission (2007) *Investigation into the Service for People with Learning Disabilities Provided by Sutton and Merton Primary Care Trust.* London: Healthcare Commission

Legislation, policies and reports

All UK legislation can be downloaded from www.legislation.gov.uk Policies and reports for Northern Ireland, Scotland and Wales can be found at www.northernireland.gov.uk www.scotland.gov.uk and www.wales.gov.uk respectively. Policies and reports for England can be found on the website of the relevant government department.

Adult Support and Protection (Scotland) Act 2007

Health and Social Care Act 2008

National Care Standards, Regulation of Care (Scotland) Act 2001

Safeguarding Vulnerable Groups Act 2006

Sexual Offences Act 2003

Department of Health (2008) *Safeguarding Adults: A Consultation on the Review of the 'No Secrets' Guidance.* London: Department of Health

Department of Health and Home Office (2000) *No Secrets: Guidance on developing and implementing multi-agency policies and procedures to protect vulnerable adults from abuse.* London: Department of Health (covers England)

Department of Health, Social Services and Public Safety (2010) *Adult Safeguarding in Northern Ireland, Regional and Local Partnership Arrangements.* Belfast: Department of Health, Social Services and Public Safety (covers Northern Ireland)

Office of the Public Guardian (2007) *Mental Capacity Act (2005) Code of Practice.* London: The Stationery Office

Office of the Public Guardian (2008) *Deprivation of Liberty Safeguards, Code of Practice.* London: The Stationery Office

Welsh Assembly (2000) *In Safe Hands: Implementing adult protection procedures in Wales.* Cardiff: Welsh Assembly Government

Websites

Care and Social Service Inspectorate Wales (inspection and regulation in Wales) www.csiw.wales.gov.uk

Care Quality Commission (inspection and regulation in England) www.cqc.org.uk

The Regulation and Quality Improvement Authority (Northern Ireland) www.rqia.org.uk

Independent Safeguarding Authority www.isa-gov.org.uk

Scottish Commission for the Regulation of Care (inspection and regulation in Scotland) www.carecommission.com

Skills for Care www.skillsforcare.org.uk

The Social Care Councils (responsible for the regulation and registration of social workers and other social care workers) are:

Care Council for Wales www.ccwales.org.uk

General Social Care Council (England) www.gscc.org.uk

Northern Ireland Social Care Council www.niscc.info

Scottish Social Services Council www.sssc.uk.com

Chapter 3

Knowing how to respond to suspected or alleged abuse

Following the serious case review into the murder of Steven Hoskin, Margaret Flynn who chaired the review said:

It seemed to me that every agency had a small piece of information or even quite a large piece of information, but they looked at that information as though it was disconnected from anything else. One of the principal findings of the serious case review was that every agency had a piece of a jigsaw. At no stage did they seek to discuss the piece that they held or the information, or indeed the concerns that they had about Steven's circumstances.

Margaret Flynn, Chair of the serious case review into the murder of Steven Hoskin

Introduction

The quote above highlights how important it is for people to report concerns promptly, so that information can be shared with appropriate agencies and action taken to reduce the risks to vulnerable adults.

If you suspect a person you support is being abused or neglected you have to act. Policies and procedures, both national and within your organisation, which relate to abuse and neglect state that as a social care worker supporting vulnerable adults you have a responsibility to be aware of issues to do with abuse and neglect and report any concerns or information you have that someone is, or may be, experiencing abuse.

The importance of reporting suspicions about abuse and neglect

If someone discloses or tells you about abuse that they have seen or experienced, it is clear that you have a duty to report it. However, you may think that something you have seen or heard is not that important and is not worth reporting. This is never the case. Of course, there is a risk that you or the person speaking to you have misinterpreted what you saw or heard, but there is a much greater risk that you are contributing yourself to someone's abuse by failing to report it. Even if something seems very small, when put together with information from other people it might help to show that abuse is taking place.

The individual who is being abused may not report the abuse themselves, perhaps because they are unable to communicate verbally, may be frightened, not know how to report it or not realise that they are being abused.

Your organisation's policies and procedures will stress the importance of reporting suspected abuse and neglect so that:

- the abuse can be stopped immediately;

- the perpetrator can be stopped from abusing others;

- the person who is being abused can be protected properly and receive help;

- the abuser can be held accountable for their actions and measures can be taken to prevent them abusing others, for example by referring them to the Independent Safeguarding Authority or by reporting them to the police.

Reporting suspected abuse or neglect

If someone discloses that they are experiencing abuse you must take it seriously and respond carefully.

Even if someone doesn't tell you they are experiencing abuse, you may suspect that abuse is happening because:

- you are contacted by a relative, friend, member of the public or employee of another organisation to discuss their concerns about possible abuse;

- you observe possible abuse taking place;

- you notice a number of signs or indicators that someone is being abused – you don't have to wait until you have 'hard evidence'.

Activity

Have a look at the safeguarding vulnerable adults policy and procedures in your organisation. What does it tell you about:

1. *Any immediate action you might need to take?*
2. *Whom to report allegations, suspicions or concerns of abuse to?*
3. *What you should do if your immediate line manager or supervisor is not available to give you advice?*
4. *Where to record information about your concerns and the actions you have taken?*

Then discuss the information you have found with your line manager or supervisor. If you have been unable to find the answers to any of these questions, you will need to get this information from your manager. If you are a personal assistant and your employer doesn't have detailed policies on this issue, you can still talk through with them the four questions above and note down what they advise you to do.

How, when and to whom to report suspected abuse or neglect

In your induction as a learning disability worker you will learn about the importance of confidentiality. However, reporting information about suspected abuse does not breach confidentiality and you must not keep it to yourself. If someone tells you that they suspect a person you support is being abused, you must make it clear to them that you have to report it in accordance with your organisation's policies and procedures regarding adult protection. You must report your concerns even if you think that the person who told you their concerns might be unhappy about it. Your policies and procedures will advise you to report abuse to your line manager in the first instance. It will be their responsibility to make sure that the person or people who are at risk of abuse are kept safe.

The following flowchart provides a summary of the main responsibilities of people providing direct care and support.

Ensure immediate safety
If necessary contact emergency services, e.g. police or ambulance.
Does the person need to be moved from a dangerous environment?
Do not put yourself in danger.

Preserve evidence
Do not touch or move anything unless absolutely necessary.
Consider if there are any items that might be needed as evidence.
Do not ask leading questions (putting words in people's mouths) as this contaminates evidence.
Do not confront the alleged abuser or accuse anyone of committing abuse.

Report
Report to your supervisor or line manager at the earliest possible opportunity (but always within 24 hours).
If your line manager is unavailable, or if you suspect your line manager may be involved in the abuse, report to a more senior manager.
If you are unable to contact a senior manager you can report your concerns directly to the local authority social services department.

Record
Make a clear, factual record of all the details – what you saw, what the person said (in their own words), and the environment.
All records must be signed and state time and date that the record was completed, along with the time and date of any disclosures or incidents.
Ensure all records are legible and written in black ink if possible (to allow records to be photocopied if necessary).

You work in a supported living service for people with learning disabilities, and as part of your job you provide support to Jane. She is 30 and lives in her own flat. She has four hours of support each day, but manages independently the rest of the time.

One day you call to visit and when Jane lets you in you notice that she has a cut on her lip and a large bruise next to her right eye. Jane notices that you have seen these injuries and she tells you that she had a bit of an argument with her boyfriend last night, but that everything is OK now.

Think about the four points in the previous flowchart and how each of these would influence what you would do.

When you have written down your thoughts and ideas, please discuss these with your supervisor or manager.

It is not enough just to pass on the information you have received verbally. You must make a written record of what you have seen or been told as soon as possible after the incident. This is because verbal information can be misinterpreted by the person you are passing it on to. If you do not record the information soon after the event you may find that you forget some details or that you do not remember exactly what you saw or were told. You should write down the following.

It is not enough just to pass on information you have received verbally, you must make a written record of what you have seen or been told.

- When the incident took place or when you were told about the incident.

- Who was involved and the names of other witnesses, including other people supported by your organisation, colleagues, visitors and family members.

- A description of what you saw or were told, making sure that you include as much detail as you can and that you record the facts and not your own views or opinions about what you saw, for example:

  I saw Joseph trip up and drop the drinks tray. I heard Brenda say to Joseph 'Now you've been naughty you can't have a drink.' NOT 'Brenda was really annoyed with Joseph and told him off'.

- Any other information that might be relevant, for example if there are any previous events which gave you cause for concern.

When?	When did the incident take place?
Who?	Who was involved?
What?	What did you see or were you told?
Where?	Where did the incident happen?

The four areas to consider when making a written record.

What happens after you have reported your concerns?

Once you have reported your concerns to your line manager, they will then decide whether or not to make a referral under the local multi-agency safeguarding adults procedures. They would make a decision not to make a referral only if there was a definite explanation for the concern that did not involve abuse. For example, you might have reported seeing a large bruise when you have been supporting someone to get dressed, and your manager then checked the accident records and discovered that the bruising is the result of a fall that has been followed up (the person has been checked by doctor, the risk assessment has been reviewed, etc.). If, however, your manager still has concerns that the situation might or does involve abuse or neglect (i.e. they do not have to be 100 per cent certain), they would make a referral.

The usual process would then involve your line manager reporting through the local authority contact centre, call centre or central duty team (different terms are used in each area). The referral is then passed on to a social work or care management team and a lead investigating officer is appointed – this will often be a social worker – although the police will take the lead in criminal investigations. A multi-agency strategy meeting will be held to plan the investigation and any other actions that are required to safeguard the vulnerable person.

Responding to a disclosure of abuse

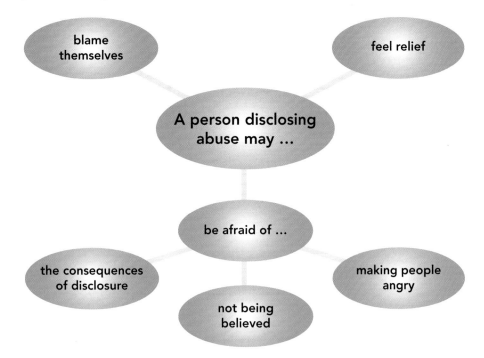

'Disclosure' is the term that is commonly used when an abused person tells someone about the abuse. It is most often associated with sexual abuse, but can also refer to other forms of abuse.

When someone makes a disclosure about abuse they are likely to experience a whole range of feelings. It is important for you to understand the difficulty that disclosure presents for someone with learning disabilities. The person raising the concern is likely to experience a great deal of fear and confusion and a whole range of other feelings. Being aware of how the person might be feeling puts you in a much better position to listen and to provide the support the individual will need throughout the disclosure period and beyond. It is also important that members of the individual's family are also aware of these issues so that they also respond appropriately to a disclosure of abuse.

As a support worker you should take action in response to a disclosure of abuse from a person you support. There are also things you should avoid doing.

Actions to take following a disclosure of abuse

If someone discloses abuse to you it can be difficult to know what to say or do, especially if you are a new or inexperienced worker. It's important to think carefully about your actions so that you support the individual, while at the same time making sure that your actions do not put any future investigation at risk.

Supporting the individual

A person with a learning disability who is disclosing abuse is likely to experience a range of feelings that might include:

- blaming themselves;
- being afraid of the consequences of the disclosure;
- being afraid of not being believed;
- being afraid of making people angry;
- relief at the disclosure.

Thinking point

Have you ever been worried about something for a long time without telling anyone? Whom did you choose to talk to? How did you feel when you had told them?

Staff must be trained to know and properly follow their organisation's policies and procedures on the reporting and recording of suspected abuse.

It is not easy to support someone who discloses abuse, especially if you have no previous experience of doing so. Here are some practical steps you can take.

- You may need to set aside some time immediately to talk to the person. This means you may have to delay another activity or, if the disclosure occurred near the end of your shift, be prepared to work late.

- Try to stay calm and not to show any feelings you may have, such as shock, anger or disgust. The individual may think that they are upsetting you and not tell you any more.

- Think carefully about what you say. Avoid expressions such as 'you're joking!', or expressing any opinion about what you are being told.

- Reassure the person that:
  - the disclosure will be taken seriously;
  - they are not to blame and that the abuse is not their fault;
  - the disclosure was the right thing to do.

- Listen carefully and try not to interrupt when someone is telling you their story. Reflect back to the person what they have told you to check that you have understood. If they change their version of events during the discussion you should report both versions.

- Explain clearly to the person what will happen next, for example that you will speak to your line manager, with or without the individual present, depending on how they feel. Your manager will then want to hear about the abuse themselves when the person feels ready to talk about it again. Reassure them that you will be there if that's what they want.

- Explain that you and your line manager will make sure that the abuse is dealt with and that it will stop. Be honest with the individual concerned, saying that it might take time to get everything done and that they might have to speak to some other people, but that you will be there to help whenever they need you.

- Check that the person understands what you have said. You may have to repeat it several times as they may be very emotional and be unable to take in what you are saying at first.

- While you are talking to the person, observe their behaviour and body language. Look for other indicators, for example whether they appear frightened or upset.

Following your organisation's policy and procedures

If someone discloses abuse to you, you must follow your organisation's policies and procedures, or the guidance from your employer if you are a personal assistant, carefully. This includes:

- completing the records required clearly and accurately;

- remembering to include the time and date, and to sign the report;

- raising the concern about abuse to the correct person, usually your line manager.

Remember your role is to report the abuse. You must not try to carry out your own investigation.

Actions to avoid following a disclosure of abuse

There are a number of actions you should avoid when someone discloses abuse. You could compromise the situation and make it impossible for the concern to be properly investigated. This is even more important if the concern might lead to a criminal investigation.

Unfortunately, people with learning disabilities are already considered to be unreliable witnesses in law. If you ask questions about the abuse, you may be seen as having put ideas in their mind or convinced them that they have been abused. If this happens it is unlikely that the investigation can proceed. As it is difficult for cases of the abuse of people with learning disabilities to get to court, support workers or members of the person's family will need guidance about how to behave to make sure they do not accidentally weaken the case. The way you ask questions is important. You must make sure that you do not 'suggest' to the individual who has disclosed abuse what might have happened or how they might be feeling. For example, instead of saying 'Who gave you that bruise?', you could say 'Would you like to tell me how you got that bruise?' Or, instead of saying 'Did he touch you? That's awful. You must feel dreadful', you could say 'What happened? How are you feeling?'

Responding to a disclosure of abuse

The following are some of the kinds of things you should avoid saying when someone discloses abuse. Write down what you think you should say instead.

- *It looks as though someone has upset you. Who was it?*
- *Do you think John could have taken your money?*
- *Who made you cry?*
- *That's a big bruise. Who hit you?*
- *Has Sheila been calling you names again?*
- *I bet that has really upset you – has it?*

Discuss your answers with your supervisor or line manager.

In 2001, Mencap, Respond and VOICE produced a joint document relating to the law and the abuse of people with learning disabilities. In it they said:

> People with a learning disability who have been sexually abused do not receive equal and just treatment within the legal system… Few cases reach court and even fewer result in conviction.
>
> *Behind Closed Doors: Preventing sexual abuse against adults with a learning disability.* London, Mencap, 2001

Change happens slowly. In 2005, the charity Action on Elder Abuse undertook government funded research into the abuse of vulnerable adults. They found that out of 639 cases referred to adult protection teams in nine local authorities over a six month period, only five resulted in prosecution. Therefore, although it is important that you listen and reassure a person disclosing abuse, it is essential not to ask any leading questions about the alleged abuse.

In 2008 the Commission for Social Care Inspection published a report titled *Safeguarding Adults: A study of the effectiveness of arrangements to safeguard adults from abuse.* It reported that, on average, councils had reported increases in safeguarding referrals of 36 per cent from the previous year. However, in councils taking part in the study, annual increases in referrals ranged from 10 to 150 per cent, reflecting (in part) varied practice in raising awareness of abuse and the steps to take. This demonstrates that increased awareness is leading to a higher number of concerns and suspicions being reported than previously.

In addition, there are now facilities to assist vulnerable people to give evidence, which is beginning to change the traditional view that most vulnerable adults would be unreliable witnesses in court (which contributed to the low number of cases taken through the criminal justice system). The Youth Justice and Criminal Evidence Act 1999 makes provision across the UK for vulnerable or intimidated witnesses to be eligible for 'Special Measures'.

A vulnerable adult or intimidated witness is defined as someone who:

- is under the age of 17 at the time of the hearing;
- suffers from a mental disorder within the meaning of the Mental Health Act 1983, or who has a significant impairment of intelligence or social functioning, or who has a physical disability or disorder;
- a witness whose evidence, in the opinion of the court, is likely to be diminished by fear or distress about testifying.

The 'Special Measures' include:

- screening witnesses from the accused;
- evidence by live link;
- support from a trained intermediary before, during and after the proceedings;
- evidence given in private, i.e. clearing the court;
- removal of wigs and gowns;
- video-recorded evidence;
- video-recorded cross-examination or re-examination;
- examination of witnesses through an intermediary;
- aids to communication.

Despite these positive developments, there are still a large number of cases of abuse of vulnerable adults (that involve suspected crimes), which do not go to court. Therefore, it is essential that you do everything you can to obtain an accurate, factual picture of the allegation, whilst avoiding the contamination of evidence.

Be very careful not to express anger, not even towards the perpetrator, as the person who has disclosed abuse may think you are angry with them. Do not display any disbelief, as this may undermine the person making the disclosure.

You must not confront the alleged abuser because this is the responsibility of the investigating authorities and you may be giving them time to confront or intimidate the victim, or destroy the evidence. If the case goes to a criminal investigation you will be questioned and may also be required to act as a witness. Any attempt to discuss the abuse with the perpetrator will endanger the investigation.

You should not discuss the alleged or suspected abuse with colleagues, apart from those involved in the same way as yourself, or the person's family, or your own friends or family. This is a time when confidentiality is paramount. You are likely to need support yourself at this time. A more experienced senior worker in your organisation should take on responsibility for supporting family carers and you and your colleagues. You should not deal with this on your own.

In the case of alleged recent sexual abuse, discourage the person from washing, bathing or cleaning their teeth as they may be removing evidence. The police will tell the person when they can wash and change their clothing. You should also leave any other evidence until the police arrive. For example you should not tidy or clean the area where the incident is alleged to have taken place.

Sadly, incidents of alleged abuse make good stories for the press, and journalists from your local newspaper, radio or TV station may try to contact your organisation. If your organisation has a media policy you should familiarise yourself with it and pass on any enquiries from the press to the appropriate person.

Responding to suspicion of abuse of a child

Although you may not work directly with children, you have a duty to report any suspicions you have that any child that you come across in the course of your work is being abused or neglected, not just those with a learning disability.

The protection of children is covered separately as a result of legislation following a number of high profile cases where children were abused and services failed to protect them.

The Children Act 2004 (England and Wales) amends the Children Act 1989 and places a duty on local authorities and their partners (including the police, health service providers and the youth justice system) to cooperate to promote the wellbeing of children and young people and to make arrangements to safeguard and promote the welfare of children. Separate legislation applies in Scotland – the Children (Scotland) Act 1995, and in Northern Ireland – the Children (Northern Ireland) Order 1995.

One of the outcomes from the common induction standards which relates to abuse and neglect is that all new employees should know what to do if they suspect any child is being abused or neglected.

If you suspect any child is being abused, you should follow your organisation's usual policies and procedures for reporting abuse. Your line manager will refer your report to the local authority child protection team, who will decide what action should be taken. Further information about the role of the child protection team in your area can be found on your local authority's website.

When further information is needed

You may find yourself in a situation in which you think abuse might be occurring but you are not sure. For example:

- when you observe a colleague treating someone they are supporting in a way which seems to you to be abusive, but you are not sure;

- when you are not sure whether an action you have taken or plan to take might be considered to be abusive;

- when a friend of someone you support suggests in a very roundabout way that their money may be being used by other members of their family or someone else they know.

If you need further information or advice you should be able to get this from your line manager, the organisation's policies and procedures, or independent regulators such as the Care Quality Commission.

Note: the Care Quality Commission is the independent regulator for Health and Social Care in England. The regulators for Wales, Scotland and Northern Ireland are listed at the end of **Chapter 2**.

Key points from this chapter

- Always take allegations seriously and report them to your manager.

- You must report all concerns, even if you are not sure whether they are linked to abuse and neglect.

- Reporting information about suspected abuse does not breach confidentiality – you must not keep it to yourself.

- Your main responsibilities are to ensure immediate safety, preserve evidence, report and record.

- Record the facts – what you saw and what you heard – not what you think might have happened.

- If someone discloses abuse to you, you will need to support the individual while also making sure your actions do not put any future investigation at risk.

- It is your job to report your concerns, but not to investigate – this will be co-ordinated through the local multi-agency procedures.

- Remember – you also have a duty to report any concerns or suspicions of abuse to children.

- Disclosures of abuse do not breach confidentiality. It is your duty to report your own suspicions of abuse or any information given to you by another person.

References and where to go for more information

Commission for Social Care Inspection (now Care Quality Commission) (2008) *Safeguarding Adults: A study of the effectiveness of arrangements to safeguard adults from abuse.* London: CSCI

Mencap (2001) *Behind Closed Doors.* London: Mencap (available at www.mencap.org.uk)

Legislation, policies and reports

All UK legislation can be downloaded from www.legislation.gov.uk Policies and reports for Northern Ireland, Scotland and Wales can be found at www.northernireland.gov.uk www.scotland.gov.uk and www.wales.gov.uk respectively. Policies and reports for England can be found on the website of the relevant government department.

Children Act 2004 (England and Wales)

Children (Northern Ireland) Order 1995

Children (Scotland) Act 1995

Youth Justice and Criminal Evidence Act 1999

Websites

Action on Elder Abuse www.elderabuse.org.uk

Mencap www.mencap.org.uk

Respond www.respond.org.uk

Skills for Care www.skillsforcare.org.uk

VOICE UK www.voiceuk.org.uk

Chapter 4

Understanding ways to reduce the likelihood of abuse

> Bill used to find it hard to talk about some of the things he had been through, so I told him it might help if he wrote his feelings down on paper. He did this and put his writings in a drawer in his bedroom.
>
> He told the person supporting him not to go in his bedroom because it was his private space.
>
> One day the support worker phoned me and said she had found some letters in Bill's drawer that worried her. I asked her which drawer and she said the one in his bedroom. I knew that this was Bill's private space, so I told her she had no right going in there, and also she had no right talking to me about the letters without asking Bill.
>
> I told Bill what had happened and he took it up with the manager of the service. He got someone else to support him, who he felt would respect his privacy.
>
> *Karen Flood, describing a situation that happened to her and Bill Heron.*

Introduction

This story illustrates how important it is for people to understand their rights. In this example, Karen and Bill clearly understood their rights, so they were able to take appropriate action to challenge the actions of the support worker. Not everyone is aware of their rights, and this can leave them more open to abuse.

It is important to have clear policies and procedures in place to respond quickly and appropriately to concerns, suspicions and disclosures of abuse. However, it is far better to have policies and systems in place which prevent abuse from occurring in the first place.

Reducing the vulnerability of individuals with learning disabilities

Although we have seen that people with learning disabilities are sometimes more vulnerable to abuse and neglect, there are many ways in which you can work in partnership with people with learning disabilities and their families to reduce their vulnerability. Here are some of the ways you can do this.

- Help people understand that they have the right to control their own lives and to make their own choices and decisions, for example to make small daily choices such as what to eat and what to wear, as well as major decisions about where to live and whom to live with.

Help people to understand that they have the right to control their own lives and make choices and decisions.

- Challenge situations, circumstances and people who use their power negatively, for example when people with learning disabilities are harassed or bullied by strangers, segregated or barred from establishments, insulted or ignored.

- Give people information they need in a form that they can understand so that they become aware of their rights and choices, for example about sex and sexuality.

- Support people to develop the skills they need to stand up for their rights, for example assertiveness training.

- Support people to access other sources of help or information, for example an advocate or local advocacy group.

It is important that you give people information about their rights. An increasing number of people with learning disabilities are purchasing support through direct payments or individual budgets. While this gives people more choice and control, there is potentially less monitoring and regulation than with traditional services. Therefore, it is essential that people are clear about the standard of support they should expect, and that they know what they can do if they are not happy with this.

People with complex needs may require information in a range of different formats, making sure their communication needs are met.

Give people information they need in a form they can understand so that they become aware of their rights and choices.

People from black and minority ethnic groups may not always access traditional services for information, such as libraries. We need to consider where the best places are to provide information about people's rights so they can access this easily. We need to make sure that information and support are sensitive to people's cultural and religious needs and wishes.

The Dignity Challenge

In 2006 the Dignity in Care Campaign was launched. The following provides a summary of the main features.

High-quality services that respect people's dignity should:

1. Have a zero tolerance of all forms of abuse.

2. Support people with the same respect you would want for yourself or a member of your family.

3. Treat each person as an individual by offering a personalised service.

4. Enable people to maintain the maximum possible level of independence, choice and control.

5. Listen and support people to express their needs and wants.

6. Respect people's right to privacy.

7. Ensure people feel able to complain without fear of retribution.

8. Engage with family members and carers as care partners.

9. Assist people to maintain confidence and a positive self-esteem.

10. Act to alleviate people's loneliness and isolation.

By providing support in this way you will be helping to prevent abuse and mistreatment of vulnerable adults.

Person centred values

In Chapter 1 there is a description of vulnerability being linked to dependence, lack of control and lack of power. Person centred working promotes independence and encourages people to have as much control over their lives as possible, which then leads to reduced vulnerability.

Person centred working promotes independence and encourages people to have as much control over their lives as possible, which then leads to reduced vulnerability.

You can find out a lot more about person centred support in the book *Person Centred Approaches when Supporting People with a Learning Disability* in this series.

Active participation

Active participation is a way of working that recognises an individual's right to participate in the activities and relationships of everyday life as independently as possible; the individual is regarded as an active partner in their own support, rather than a passive recipient.

Activity

Two workers are involved in supporting Gill, a woman with a moderate level of learning disabilities. One member of staff always seems to be in a rush and when Gill needs some shopping, she always says, 'I'll just take some of your money and nip to the supermarket to get the same things that you usually get'. The other member of staff makes a point of supporting Gill to do her own shopping. She encourages Gill to decide where to go, what to buy and how much to spend, and she always insists on Gill keeping hold of her own money to pay for the shopping.

In what ways do you think the first member of staff's approach may make Gill more vulnerable to abuse?

Think about the way you provide support. Do you always provide support in a way that encourages people to be actively involved and to make their own choices and decisions?

Discuss your ideas with your supervisor or manager.

Prevention of abuse

You will find the ideas listed below helpful in thinking about ways that you and your colleagues can work to reduce possible abuse.

- Zero tolerance of abuse and neglect within the organisation.
- Effective leadership.
- Open management style.
- Flexible routines and regimes.
- Robust recruitment and selection procedures that involve people with a learning disability and family carers (including Criminal Record Bureau and Independent Safeguarding Authority checks).

- Regular team meetings where staff are encouraged to discuss problems, issues and difficulties.

- Regular and effective staff supervision.

- Well publicised and effective policies and procedures (e.g. safeguarding adults, complaints, behaviour support, disciplinary and capability, equal opportunities, physical intervention, medication, finance, risk assessment and management).

- Appropriate and varied skills mix of staff.

- Regular and effective staff training and development opportunities (e.g. positive behaviour support, communication, personal relationships and sexuality, anti-oppressive practice).

- Support offered to staff members that are stressed, e.g. occupational health and counselling.

- Conduct return to work interviews following sickness absence.

- Conduct exit interviews to discover reasons for staff leaving.

- Regular audits and quality assurance mechanisms.

In relation to the people you support

- Individualised care or support plans (involving the people you support in developing and reviewing these regularly).

- Development of person centred approaches.

- Involvement of people who use services in the planning and delivery of these services, e.g. residents' meetings, people with learning disabilities on planning groups.

- Good partnerships with relatives and friends.

- Regular reviews of medication.

- Development of more imaginative ways of managing complex and challenging behaviour.

- Assessment of capacity to make decisions, rather than making assumptions about this.

- Involvement of specialist services (e.g. speech and language therapy, psychology) as appropriate.

- Independent advocacy and self-advocacy schemes.

Accessible complaints procedures

It is important to recognise the importance of complaints as a valuable form of feedback about the service and the support you provide. This helps to constantly improve services.

A complaint is a way of someone letting us know that they are not happy with a particular service. It is important that complaints procedures are easy for people to follow so they can tell us if:

- they think we have done something wrong;

- we have not done something that we said we would do;

- they are not satisfied with a particular service or set of services that we provide.

A complaints procedure should provide clear information about:

- whom to contact to make the complaint;

- support available to make the complaint (for example, use of an advocate);

- what people should expect with regard to the response, timescale, etc.;

- whom to go to if they are unhappy with the response (e.g. local government ombudsman).

Complaints procedures can help to empower people, by providing them with the opportunity to describe what they feel is wrong and what they think should happen to address this. If complaints are investigated and responded to promptly and effectively, this can avoid major problems building up. Abuse is far less likely to happen in services that are open to scrutiny, and where the people receiving support and family carers are actively encouraged to provide feedback.

Most services now have policies with titles such as 'customer feedback' or 'compliments and complaints'. This is because it is also important to encourage people to provide positive feedback, to let us know when we are getting things right.

You can find out more about accessible complaints from *Hearing from the Seldom Heard*, downloadable from www.bild.org.uk

Activity

Have a look at the complaints (or compliments and complaints) policy and procedure within your organisation. Is it easy to follow; is it accessible? Would the people you support and their family members be able to understand the policy without help? Does it contain clear information about what people should expect when they make a complaint? Does it include a statement to reassure people that complaints are seen in a positive light, to help improve services, rather than making the person feel that they are being a nuisance?

When you have read the policy and considered these points, discuss your views with your supervisor or manager.

Key points from this chapter

- It is important to help the people you support to understand their rights, so they will become more able to speak up for themselves.

- The support you provide must respect and promote people's dignity.

- The organisation should have a zero tolerance of abuse.

- Promoting person centred values leads to things being done in the way that the person you support wants them to be done.

- Person centred working promotes independence and encourages people to have as much control over their lives as possible, which can reduce vulnerability to abuse.

- The people you support should be seen as active partners in their support, rather than as passive recipients.

- Complaints procedures need to be accessible and people should feel comfortable in using these to express their views.

References and where to go for more information

References

Routledge, M, Sanderson, H and Greig, R (2002) *Planning with People: Towards Person Centred Approaches.* London: Department of Health

Websites

NHS (2006) *Dignity in Care Campaign* www.dignityincare.org.uk

Chapter 5

Knowing how to recognise and report unsafe practices

A few years ago I was working as a charge nurse and one of the patients on the ward told me that a nurse who worked on nights had slapped her across the face. I reported this to the nursing officer and there was an investigation. The nurse who worked on nights was suspended. Her colleagues were very unhappy about me having reported the allegation and would say things like – how could you report one of your own? I explained that I had simply passed on an allegation to be investigated, according to the procedures. Because I was senior to these staff it just made me feel slightly uncomfortable, but afterwards I thought that if I had been a nursing assistant they could have made life really hard for me.

During the investigation other people came forward eventually and reported things that they had seen the night nurse doing – swearing at patients, threatening them and pushing them around. She ended up being dismissed, but still some of the night staff saw me as a trouble maker. I was convinced I had done the right thing because I felt I had helped to prevent further abuse of vulnerable people.

Health service manager

Introduction

People who speak out about bad practices in the workplace are commonly known as 'whistleblowers'. Their actions draw attention to what is happening and hopefully make sure that it stops. A whistleblower is someone who reports bad practices to higher authorities or to people who have the power to investigate and put a stop to those practices. There are whistleblowers in all areas of employment. Most instances of whistleblowing go unnoticed. Many people think they are just doing their job when they report that something is going wrong, and mostly their concerns are addressed. However, sometimes whistleblowers make the news headlines. An example from social care is that in February 2006 a whistleblower exposed alleged abuse at a care home for people with severe learning disabilities in Hertfordshire, which made national headlines. The whistleblower was a senior support worker. As a result of raising his concerns both the county council and the care provider investigated the issues fully and then ensured measures were put in place to address all the issues involved.

Learning outcomes

This chapter looks at:

- why the safety and wellbeing of individuals who are being supported must always take priority over other considerations;

- examples of unsafe practices that may affect the wellbeing of individuals;

- the actions to take if unsafe practices have been identified;

- the action to take if suspected abuse or unsafe practices have been reported but nothing has been done in response.

This chapter covers:

- Level 2 and level 3 HSC 024 level 2 – Principles of safeguarding and protection: Learning Outcome 5

Why the safety of people comes first

In society, we all have a moral responsibility to look after one another. However, in your role as a learning disability worker this is formalised and you are said to have a 'duty of care' to the people you support. What this means in practice is that the safety of the people you support must take priority over everything else.

While employees have a responsibility to report abuse or bad practices, there is evidence from people who have done this that in practice it can be a very difficult thing to do. Whistleblowers may fear the consequences for themselves from individuals or organisations they are reporting on. If the alleged abuser is a colleague, the whistleblower may be afraid that other colleagues will be hostile towards them or isolate them:

I felt like I'd done something wrong because nobody would speak to me on the unit.

Whistleblower, reported in research paper, *Blowing the whistle on the abuse of adults with learning disabilities*, Rebecca Calcraft, 2005.

The whistleblower may fear reprisals from the organisation if the matter they reported on was about organisational procedures or practices. For example, they may fear that they might be moved to a different or more challenging work setting or that they may be subject to bullying or harassment.

People who are considering reporting serious cases of abuse or bad practices should be aware that their own lives, the lives of the individuals they support and their colleagues could be disrupted while an investigation is carried out.

However, people also need to seriously consider the consequences of failing to report concerns. Things could continue to get worse, people with learning disabilities could be harmed, and the person with the concerns could get into even more trouble in the long run due to their failure to fulfil their duty of care.

Although reporting abuse, neglect or bad practice can be difficult, there is a law that protects whistleblowers. This is the Public Interest Disclosure Act 1998 or 'Whistleblowers Act', which encourages people to speak out about bad practice in the workplace and protects them from victimisation and dismissal for raising their concerns. It protects employees who raise concerns 'in good faith' (i.e. that their concern is genuine and not malicious) and states that if an employee is victimised as a result of their concern they can bring a claim for compensation to an employment tribunal.

Organisations are encouraged to put in place a 'whistleblowing policy' to protect their employees. It's a good idea to make the families of the individuals you are supporting aware of the whistleblowing policy so they know that staff will be protected if they speak out about abuse.

Thinking point

Have you ever spoken out about something that you believed to be wrong, either in your personal life or at work? Did you think carefully before you did it? How did you feel?

Public Concern at Work is a charity that was set up to provide advice, guidance and support to whistleblowers. The website (www.pcaw.co.uk) gives information about a number of cases where whistleblowers felt they had achieved positive outcomes by reporting concerns, and also gives examples of whistleblowers receiving compensation because they were unfairly treated by their employers for reporting concerns.

Unsafe practices

In the first chapter we looked at types of abuse and the signs and symptoms associated with these. Generally speaking, an employee should report any incidents of abuse using their organisation's safeguarding adults policy. However, there may be situations which do not appear to fit into the categories of abuse which were described in that chapter, but which occur over a period of time, and which the worker may feel uncomfortable about. These are described as 'unsafe practices', and should also be reported.

Examples of unsafe practices are:

- workers who are poorly trained or untrained in specialist areas, for example in working with people with autism, in supporting people with behaviour that could be called challenging or in administering medication;

- where staffing levels are very low, for example where a person who uses the services presents behaviour that is considered challenging and the staffing level is below the level that was agreed to keep that person and others safe;

- an organisation employing staff to 'sleep in' in a service when the person who is being supported should have a worker who is awake at night, for example because of their health needs;

- two of the personal assistants in a team supporting a person are habitually late for work, compromising the safety of the individual they support.

Resource and operational difficulties

Abuse can occur because workers are not properly trained or have got into sloppy or poor ways of working. This can sometimes be because of inadequate supervision or management.

Activity

Read through the following scenarios and then consider whether you feel they involve unsafe practice, and what you would do if you were faced with these situations.

- *The manager of a service asks a support worker to take Sam out to the shops on their own. The support plan and risk assessment specify that two members of staff must be present at all times when Sam is out, due to him sometimes having difficulty controlling his behaviour when he gets stressed. When the support worker questions this, the manager says, 'I know it says that, but Sam has been OK all week and if you don't take him he won't be able to go out'.*

- *A personal assistant is providing support to Suzi, who lives in her own home. Suzi has mobility difficulties and a hoist is needed to move her from the bed to her wheelchair. This is clearly recorded in Suzi's care plan and moving and handling risk assessment. The personal assistant notices that one of the bolts in the hoist is loose and reports this to Suzi's mother, who manages her direct payment and supervises the personal assistants. Suzi's mother advises her to carry on using the hoist, but says that if they are not comfortable with this they will just have to lift her from the bed to her wheelchair.*

- *A senior care worker is on night duty in a residential unit. One of the people who live in the unit, Surjinder, has become very upset and keeps hitting himself in the face and scratching his arms, to the point where they are bleeding. The senior care worker phones the on-call manager for advice, and they advise them to administer some sedative medication. The senior care worker informs the manager that Surjinder had the maximum prescribed dose of their medication three hours ago and, therefore, it is too soon to give him any more yet. The manager tells the senior care worker to give another dose of the medication, but to record that it was given three hours later, so it doesn't look like too much has been given.*

When you have considered what you would do in these situations, discuss your views with your supervisor or manager or a senior colleague.

Examples of resource and operational difficulties which should be reported are:

- visits or details of support given not being recorded accurately;

- neglecting individuals who have communication difficulties, for example 'forgetting' to offer someone who has profound learning disabilities a drink because they are not able to communicate their needs and wishes verbally;

- neglecting the hygiene of the person's environment, or leaving jobs for colleagues to do, for example leaving damp or soiled sheets on a bed in the morning so that the worker supporting the person when they go to bed has to change them;

Good management will ensure staff are properly trained and this is likely to reduce difficulties in the running of the service.

- equipment or aids that are unsuitable or even dangerous, for example wheelchairs or hoists that are not appropriate for the needs of the person;

- poor management or inadequate training, leading to difficulties in the running of the service.

How to report unsafe practices

Most policies will suggest that you report your concerns in the first instance to your line manager or, if your line manager is implicated by the concern you have raised, to a senior manager within the organisation. In most cases the manager will be pleased that you have reported your concerns and will take action informally to make sure the bad practices stop. However, as we have seen, reporting a serious case of bad practice can be a very difficult thing to do and can have serious consequences for the organisation and all the people involved.

Before you raise your concerns, you should think carefully about what might happen as a result of your actions. You should also remember that you are a 'witness', reporting something that has happened to somebody else, not to you. This means that your role is only to report your concerns, not to investigate them. You should not use the whistleblowing policy to pursue a personal grievance. If you feel that you have been badly treated by your employer, you will need to follow your organisation's grievance procedure, not the whistleblowing policy.

Most whistleblowing policies suggest that you may like to seek the advice and support of someone independent before you raise your concern. For example, the organisation Public Concern at Work offers free advice to people who have raised, or are considering raising, concerns, and they can offer more help if they are contacted at an early stage. You might also contact your union representative, someone from your personnel department or simply ask a friend to offer you support, but without discussing confidential details such as the names of the people involved or the work setting.

Activity

Read a copy of the whistleblowing policy for your organisation and check that you understand it. How and to whom should you report any concerns about abuse, neglect or unsafe work practices?

Discuss the policy with your line manager if there are any points you are unclear about.

What to do if nothing is done

If you have followed your organisation's procedures to report abuse, neglect, unsafe practices or operational difficulties, and you feel that nothing has been done or nothing changes, then most whistleblowing policies advise you to report your concerns to an external body. For people who work in learning disability services in England this is probably the Care Quality Commission (CQC), which is likely to regulate the service you work in. If you work in a regulated service in Northern Ireland, Wales or Scotland you need to contact the relevant regulator authority. This is a very serious step to take. You should make sure you seek independent advice before you do this. As a witness you would not have been kept informed about the progress or outcome of any investigation that has taken place, and you should bear in mind that actions may have been taken without your knowledge.

If a support worker or volunteer feels their manager (and possibly more senior managers) is not taking a matter seriously, or is actually involved in the abuse, they have the right to report their concerns to:

- the contact point identified within the local multi-agency safeguarding adults policy (usually the local authority);
- the Care Quality Commission (or the appropriate regulator for the country you work in);
- the police if there is any suspicion that a crime has been or will be committed.

They should also keep a diary of their concerns and all the actions they have taken in relation to these (whom they have contacted, when they contacted them, what response they got).

Key points from this chapter

- You have a duty of care to report abuse – this means that the safety of the people you support must always come first.

- Whistleblowing can be difficult, but remember that if you fail to report concerns you could be allowing abuse to continue.

- Whistleblowers who follow the correct procedures will be protected from victimisation by the law.

- Lack of resources and poor practice can lead to abuse and these need to be addressed promptly and effectively.

- You need to have a clear knowledge of how to report abuse through safeguarding procedures, and a good understanding of the whistleblowing policy in your organisation so you know what to do and whom to go to if necessary.

- It is your responsibility to report unsafe practices. Although this may be difficult, you are protected by the law.

References and where to go for more information

References

Calcraft, R (2005) *Blowing the Whistle on the Abuse of Adults with Learning Disabilities.* Nottingham: Ann Craft Trust (available at www.anncrafttrust.org)

Legislation, policies and reports

All UK legislation can be downloaded from www.legislation.gov.uk
Policies and reports for Northern Ireland, Scotland and Wales can be found at www.northernireland.gov.uk www.scotland.gov.uk and www.wales.gov.uk respectively. Policies and report for England can be found on the website of the relevant government department.

Public Interest Disclosure Act 1998 ('Whistleblowers Act')

Websites

Public Concern at Work www.pcaw.co.uk

Glossary

Abuse – a violation of a person's human and civil rights by any other person or persons, which usually involves a misuse of power.

Adult – a person aged 18 years or over.

Challenging behaviour – behaviour which puts the safety of the person or others at risk or has a significant impact on the person's or other people's quality of life.

Code of conduct – a document provided by an organisation setting out the standards that staff are expected to work to.

Code of practice – a document for social care workers setting out the standards they should work to.

Confidentiality – making sure that information is kept private and is only shared with authorised people on a need-to-know basis.

Consent – a person consents if he or she agrees by choice and has the freedom and capacity to make that choice.

Direct payments – a way for people to organise their own social care support by receiving funding direct from their council, following an assessment of their needs.

Disclosure – when an abused person tells someone about the abuse. It is most often associated with sexual abuse, but can also refer to other forms of abuse.

Duty of care – a professional responsibility to act in the best interest of the person receiving support or care.

Induction – a period of learning, shortly after starting a new job or volunteering placement, about how to provide good support to people with learning disabilities.

Legislation – laws introduced by the government, which set out people's rights and also how health and social care services should be provided.

Mental capacity – a person's ability to make their own decisions and to understand the consequences of those decisions.

Neglect – neglect means systematically and consistently failing to respond to a person's needs or failing to take actions in their best interests. It can be deliberate, but is not always done on purpose.

Personal assistants – a term often used to describe people employed directly by a person to provide care and support (e.g. through direct payments or an individual budget).

Personalisation – starting with the person as an individual with strengths, preferences and aspirations and putting them at the centre of the process of identifying their needs and making choices about how and when they are supported to live their lives.

Person centred planning – a process for continual listening and learning, focusing on what is important to someone now and in the future, and acting upon this in alliance with their family and friends.

Physical intervention – any method of responding to challenging behaviour which involves some degree of direct physical force to limit or restrict movement or mobility.

Policy – a statement or plan of action that clearly sets out an organisation's position or approach on a particular issue.

Power – the ability of a person or group of people to exercise authority over another, thereby controlling and influencing others.

Procedure – a set of instructions that sets out in detail how a policy should be put into practice and what staff should do in response to a specific situation.

Rights – a framework of laws that protects people from harm, sets out what people can say and do and guarantees the right to a fair trial and other basic entitlements, such as the right to respect, equality, etc.

Safeguarding adults – all work which helps to prevent abuse or respond to concerns, suspicions and allegations of abuse.

Staff – people employed on a paid or unpaid (voluntary) basis by an organisation to organise and deliver its services.

Vulnerable adult – a person who is or may be in need of community care services by reason of mental or other disability, age or illness and who is or may be unable to take care of themselves against significant harm or exploitation.

Whistleblower – someone who reports wrongdoing or bad practices to higher authorities.

Index

Added to a page number 'g' denotes glossary.